Love,
Pastor Larry

©2020 by Larry Briggs

All rights reserved. No portion of this book may be reproduced, stored in a retrieval system, or transmitted in any form or by any means—electronic, mechanical, photocopy, recording, scanning, or other—except for brief quotations for review or citing purposes, without the prior written permission of the author.

All Bible verses quoted New King James Version Minister's Bible

Published by Argyle Fox Publishing, argylefoxpublishing.com

Publisher holds no responsibility for content of this work. Content is the sole responsibility of the author.

ISBN 978-1-953259-00-4 (Paperback)

THE SECRET PLACE

■ ■ ■ ■ ■ ■ ■

7 Meditations for the Last-Day Church

■ ■ ■ ■ ■ ■ ■

PASTOR LARRY BRIGGS

CONTENTS

DEDICATION • 9

PREFACE • 11

SUGGESTED PLAN FOR READING • 21

MEDITATION 1
The Secret Place • 23

MEDITATION 2
The Communion of the Holy Spirit • 31

MEDITATION 3
The Difficulty of Prayer • 37

MEDITATION 4
Understanding Our Times • 53

MEDITATION 5
Signs of the Times • 61

MEDITATION 6
The Last-Day Church (New Wine) • 73

MEDITATION 7
*The Last-Day Church
(Jesus, Where Are You?)* • 83

DEDICATION

Who can find a virtuous and capable wife?
She is worth more than precious rubies.
Her husband can trust her,
And she will greatly enrich his life.
She will not hinder him but help him
All her life.
Proverbs 31:10–12

It is with deep love and appreciation that I dedicate these writings to my best friend, lifetime partner in ministry, and the most godly and supporting wife that a pastor could hope for.

Sara Jane (McCarter) Briggs

For forty-nine years you have faithfully stood by me in times of great joy and times of great sorrow. Your love, constant encouragement, and unwavering faith has been my inspiration throughout these many years. Your wisdom has been my guide through some very dark times, and your unwillingness to give up and look in a different direction has kept me in ministry. For nearly fifty years we have loved, laughed, prayed, and pastored together. You are my strength and most importantly, my best friend.

I can sincerely say that I love and respect you more now than when we first met on that stairwell at Southeastern College in Lakeland. You are, without question, the greatest gift our Heavenly Father has ever given me. You have been an invaluable partner in ministry as well as an incredible wife and mother.

Jane, from the bottom of my heart, I sincerely thank you for your continued trust, understanding, ever-growing love, and never-ending patience. Your faithfulness to our God and me and your wisdom has been a deep source of encouragement. I deeply appreciate the many unseen sacrifices that you have made to support our ministry, our family, and the churches we have been privileged to serve. Thank you most of all for believing in me and not giving up during the times that it would have been so easy to do so.

As our love continues to grow, you teach me each day the meaning of true love. I believe that through our relationship we have learned the intimacy our Heavenly Father desires from each of His children. In our walk together, we have found The Secret Place, and it is there that these meditations were birthed.

Preface

On May 5, 2017, Jane and I, along with our middle son, Bryan, sat in the office of the Director of the Psychological-Neurological Clinic at the University of Virginia Medical Center in Charlottesville, Virginia. We were there to meet with Dr. Brown to learn the results of testing I underwent four months earlier.

That day, I was diagnosed with Lewy body dementia with Parkinson's symptoms and myoclonic seizures. I have no memory of this meeting, as I'd lost my memory and the ability to care for myself.

Jane tells me that Dr. Brown compassionately revealed that LBD is a rare, terminal, incurable brain disease. Dr. Brown further explained that the average lifespan of someone with this invasive disease is two and one-half years.

Based on my testing, I'd reached the end of the spectrum.

There was nothing that could be done, so Dr. Brown suggested my family keep me as comfortable as possible and seek a full-time nursing facility equipped to handle patients with my condition. Dr. Brown then informed Jane and Bryan of the signs of deterioration to expect and suspected I had two to three weeks remaining to live.

Over the next nine days, I manifested every symptom the doctor warned my family about—except becoming combative and dying. With no memory of those painful two and a half years, I am eternally grateful to Jane for her constant care and unwavering faith. My health and cognitive abilities declined daily, but she refused to admit me into a care facility and tirelessly provided for my every need.

Three weeks passed. Then two more months. There were no signs of improvement. And then on Monday morning, July 31, 2017, I woke up totally healed with everything restored.

At some point during the night of July 30, Jesus stepped into our bedroom and healed me, restoring everything this disease had taken. Strangely, I have no memory of the two and a half years during which we battled this horrific sickness. It's like I went to bed one night and woke up two and a half years later.

After being healed, I knew I'd been sick, but I had no idea of the depth of what we—mostly Jane—went through until I read the manuscript of her book, *The Long Goodbye*. I have no doubt that without Jane's steadfast faith and the prayers of hundreds of people, I would not be writing these meditations now. I would be face to face with our Lord and Savior. But He saw fit to return me to Jane and our family and friends for a season.

We serve an awesome God who loves each of us unconditionally. In His Word, He teaches that He is omnipotent and all powerful. There is nothing He cannot do. He further reveals in His Word that it is His will that we prosper and enjoy good health. "Beloved, I pray that you may prosper in all things and be in health, just as your soul prospers." (III John 1:2) Our Heavenly Father has not only provided for our spiritual wholeness (salvation) through the sacrifice and suffering of Jesus on the Cross, but He has also paid the price for our physical and emotional healing as well.

I do want you to understand though that not all healings

are experienced in this life. God's promises are eternal and if we don't experience healing here—which we can—we certainly will in eternity. This is the foundation of our hope. He desires to bless us with blessings unimagined. He indeed is our Saviour, Healer, Holy Spirit Baptizer, Wonderful Counselor, Deliverer, and Coming King.

That said, had God not healed me, He would still be God, He would still be good, and He would still be all-powerful and loving. In fact, a dear friend died from Lewy body dementia. Was he not loved by God? Certainly he was. Was his faith insufficient? God's Word answers with a resounding, "No!" Some of the greatest saints throughout history suffered from disease and worse during their lives, finding relief only in death. (See Hebrews 11:35–40 for examples of those granted the strength to endure suffering unto death.)

Soon after I was healed and brought back from the grip of LBD, Father began revealing personal and powerful truths to my heart through His Holy Spirit. Now He instructed me to share some of these truths in these meditations.

One of the first things that He spoke to me (and I learned later that He spoke to Jane) was that my healing was for us, but the miracle was for others. He emphasized that I wasn't healed because I am a pastor nor because Jane and I have given fifty years of our lives in ministry to Him and His Church. He healed me because I am His child, and this gift is available to all of His sons and daughters.

In other words, my healing had nothing to do with who I am or what I've done, but who Jesus is and what He has done.

"Surely He has borne our griefs and carried our sorrows; Yet we esteemed Him stricken. Smitten by God, and afflicted. But He was

wounded for our transgressions, He was bruised for our iniquities; the chastisement for our peace was upon Him, and by His stripes we are healed." (Isaiah 53:4–5)

As I continued to wait upon God, seeking His purpose in all that we experienced, He directed me to reread the book of Acts, one of my favorite books in the Bible. While reading, the Holy Spirit instructed me to note every miracle, sign, and wonder performed by the disciples after the birth of the Church on the Day of Pentecost in chapter two.

As I did, He spoke this to my heart for the Church today: "I want you to understand how and why I used miracles and supernatural signs to birth my Church. I did so to show my people my deep love and care for them and to get the attention of unbelievers, to draw them to the Church to hear the saving Gospel of Jesus Christ." This echoes the end of John's Gospel:

"Now Jesus did many other signs in the presence of the disciples, which are not written in this book; but these are written so that you may believe that Jesus is the Christ, the Son of God, and that by believing you may have life in his name." (John 20:30–31)

He then revealed this prophetic word to me. "You are now living in the last days of the Church age. The 'times' of the Gentiles, as taught in Scripture, is quickly coming to an end, and I will end the Church age just as I started it—by pouring out miracles, signs, and wonders."

FROM MY HEART TO YOURS!

These are exciting days to be alive in the Kingdom of God. Biblical prophecy is being fulfilled every day before our very eyes. All that we are experiencing has been spoken by Jesus Himself in Matthew 24 and Luke 21. We should not be surprised nor fearful. The Church today has a great opportunity to impact our culture and world and to reap a harvest of souls for the Kingdom of Heaven.

People are confused, fearful, and looking for answers. The answer is only found in Jesus Christ. To accomplish the task before us, we the Church must repent and turn back to God.

"If My people who are called by My Name will humble themselves, and pray and seek My face, and turn from their wicked ways, then I will hear from Heaven, and will forgive their sin and heal their land." (II Chronicles 7:14)

As indicated in this admonition from the Lord, sin has invaded the Church. But this is nothing new. From day one, God's people have fallen for sin's enticement. (Read 1 Corinthians 5 for an example.) Today, we have culturized Christianity to the point that we equate living in America or belonging to a certain political party as making us right with God. We truly don't know right from wrong.

Without a doubt, we are living in the days the Apostle Paul spoke of in Romans 1. We have turned the truth of God into a lie and we are serving our selfish selves rather than the one who created us. We have bought into the lies of hell, believing that if it feels good, it is good.

In love I must speak the truth. If it was deemed sin in the Bible, it is still sin today. Today, as in times past, many of God's people continue to live under the influence of seducing spirits that glorify the flesh and ignore the Spirit of God.

We desperately need a Holy Spirit revival in our personal

lives and the Church. As we humble ourselves in repentance, God will respond with a mighty wave of His Spirit that will recreate an environment within the Church that will give us eyes to see and ears to hear what the Spirit is saying.

It's my heart's desire and purpose to motivate you to find your own secret place, where you can cultivate intimacy with your Heavenly Father. In Psalm 119:15, the Psalmist writes, "I will meditate on Your precepts and contemplate Your ways."

Unfortunately, we live such hurried, self-absorbed lives that we have lost all understanding of the concept of meditation. The word meditation is found 134 times in Scripture. It refers to taking time to prayerfully and intentionally focus on God and His Word. The biblical writers called it waiting upon the Lord. They spoke of it as a normal activity in their lives, used to cultivate their relationship with God. Note, with me, what Isaiah wrote:

"Have you not known? Have you not heard? The everlasting God, the Lord, the creator of the ends of the earth, neither faints nor is weary. His understanding is unsearchable. He gives power to the weak, and to those who have no might He increases strength. Even the youths shall faint and be weary, and the young men shall utterly fall, but those who wait (meditate) on the Lord shall renew their strength; they shall mount up with wings like eagles, they shall run and not be weary, they shall walk and not faint." (Isaiah 40:28–31)

They valued, as we should, the importance of being still and quiet to fully focus on God.

Simply put, meditation is the listening side of prayer. It is the practice of taking time to prayerfully and intentionally focus on a portion of God's Word to understand what it says and how it applies to our lives. It requires us to consistently create a quiet time and put our minds in neutral gear so God can speak to us personally, giving the Holy Spirit the opportunity to reveal His truth to our hearts and minds.

After my healing, the Holy Spirit instructed me to set aside a time each day to focus on God and His Word. As I have been obedient in developing this daily meditation, the Holy Spirit has deposited some powerful and personal truths in my heart.

For many Western believers, meditation is viewed as a strange, cultic activity. However, let's consider what the Apostle Paul taught in Colossians 3:16:

"Let the words of Christ dwell in you richly in all wisdom, teaching and admonishing one another in Psalms and hymns and spiritual songs, singing with grace in your hearts to the Lord."

That verse affirms meditation, and as such, should be a valued practice in the daily life of every believer.

I deeply believe that being alone with the Heavenly Father and positioning yourself to hear the Spirit is essential in becoming an overcomer in these critical days in which we now live. No doubt, prayer and meditation are the main keys in developing intimacy with our Heavenly Father. In meditation, God is able to reveal His purpose and plan for our life. Paul reinforces this truth in Romans 12:1–2:

"I beseech you therefore brethren, by the mercies of God, that you present your bodies a living sacrifice, holy and acceptable to God, which is your reasonable service. And do not be conformed to this world, but be transformed by the renewing of your mind, that you may prove what is that good and acceptable and perfect will of God."

This is a powerful, life-changing truth that many in the Church fail to comprehend. Our Heavenly Father has issued a personal invitation to each one of us, to enter His bedchamber and enjoy communion with Him.

It is my sincere prayer that as you prayerfully read these meditations you will hear directly from the Holy Spirit and that your concept of your Heavenly Father will forever change, as He reveals Himself to you through intimacy you have never known. I've experienced the treasure of cultivating intimacy with God by shutting out the noise of the world each day, and you will greatly benefit by following my example.

And a personal note to consider. Meditation is not a time to petition Father for all your needs and desires, but a time during which you intentionally wait, being still and thinking deeply. It is the practice of listening to receive a word from your Heavenly Father, to connect the dots between his revealed will (His Word) and your day-to-day life. Here, you will receive your daily bread as the Holy Spirit takes the things of God and reveals them to you (John 14:26).

Meditation doesn't require a long period of time, but the more time I spend with Him in my secret place (Psalm 91), the more of Him I desire.

As the times of the Gentiles come to a close, God is speaking to His people in prophetic revelations, opening the mysteries of His written Word, bringing clarity and understanding to our hearts and minds. Daily we are seeing the fulfillment of prophecy in the phenomenal events unfolding around the world. World leaders are stunned and shocked by these events, and fear is widespread as our lives are changed and challenged on every level. That's why it is imperative that we the Church develop the capacity to hear what the Spirit is saying. God is still in control and we can live in peace knowing that these events are clearly a part of His timeline and plan for the ages.

We are living in the most strategic time the Church has ever faced. If we set aside time daily to meditate, the Holy Spirit will reveal to each of us a wonderful secret place reserved by our Heavenly Father for all who desire fellowship with Him. In this secret place, God spoke to Moses face to face as a man speaks to his friend (Exodus 33:11) and David found forgiveness and strength to continue his ministry in Israel after failing miserably. Likewise, it will be here in this sacred place that you and I will discover all the wonderful things God has prepared for us during these difficult times.

The truths and principles in the following meditations were birthed in my secret place. I share them from my heart to yours in fervent prayer that as you deeply think (meditate) on them, you will discover your own secret place where the precious Holy Spirit will intimately reveal the Heavenly Father to you. And I pray that in developing this closeness with God, you will remain calm, stable, and expectant in these critical times.

Suggested Plan of Reading

It is my sincere prayer that these meditations will be life-changing for you, as they have been for me.

If you are like me, when you come across a book that speaks to your heart, your tendency is to dive in and read it through as quickly as possible. Sometimes you find it difficult to put down.

I certainly hope that you will share my passion as you read these meditations and that you personally discover the truths that the Holy Spirit is revealing to us in them. However, I suggest that you not rush through these, trying to consume every thought at first glance. Rather, go slowly and take the time to prayerfully consider what you are reading. The best meals are those that simmer for hours before serving, not those you get at the drive-thru. I fear that if you rush through any of these meditations, you will miss the overall message I believe the Holy Spirit is speaking to the Church today.

If read prayerful and properly, I believe this book will forever enhance your concept of God, His Church, and your involvement in it. I recommend that you read and prayerfully meditate on a single meditation each day for seven days. This may be a life-changing week that impacts you and others for the rest of your life.

It is my earnest prayer that the Holy Spirit will illuminate these truths to your hearts and minds as you spend time with Him in your secret place.

MEDITATION 1
THE SECRET PLACE

*He who dwells in the secret place of the Most High
Shall abide under the shadow of the Almighty.*
—Psalm 91:1

Come, my people, enter into your chambers, and shut your doors behind you; hide yourself, as it were, for a little moment, until the indignation is past.
—Isaiah 26:20

You and I are privileged by God to live in one of the most strategic times within His proposed plan for all ages. Prophetic events are happening on a daily basis and in the Church, our Heavenly Father is revealing Himself through the ministry of the Holy Spirit in ways we have never experienced. For all believers in the Lord Jesus Christ, these are very critical days of personal preparation and self-evaluation.

"Therefore, my beloved, as you have already obeyed, not as in my presence only, but now much more in my absence, work out your own salvation with fear and trembling; for it is God who works in you both to will and to do for his good pleasure." (Philippians 2:12)

The Secret Place

You and I were not born during this particular age by chance nor by consequence. Our Heavenly Father purposed that we be here, at this precise moment, for such a time as this. It is important that we learn to discern His voice so that we can hear what He desires for each of us in His perfect will. Jesus stressed this truth in John 10:1–5, when He said,

> *"Most assuredly, I say to you, he who does not enter the sheepfold by the door, but climbs up some other way, the same is a thief and a robber. But he who enters by the door is the shepherd of the sheep. To him the doorkeeper opens, and the sheep hear his voice; and he calls his own sheep by name and leads them out. And when he brings out his own sheep, he goes before them; and the sheep follow him, for they know his voice. Yet they will by no means follow a stranger, but will flee from him, for they do not know the voice of strangers."*

We live in a chaotic world that is full of confusing sounds. There are many voices crying out, demanding our attention. Not all of these voices are bad, but most are distracting, and we desperately need to know which ones to respond to. Jesus stressed that we know and identify His voice above all others. The only way for this to happen is to hear it often enough to readily recognize it. Therefore, it is critically important that we intentionally cultivate a personal and intimate relationship with Him through His Word, in prayer and meditation.

After my healing on July 31, 2017, the Holy Spirit spoke to my heart about a secret place that our Father has reserved for each of us. It is in this place that we develop intimacy with Him. It is here that we learn to seek the heart of our Heavenly Father and not just His hand. It is in our secret place that we learn to identify His voice, and it is here that He can share His secret plan with us.

The Apostle Paul referenced this when he wrote I Corinthians 2:6–10.

> *"However, we speak wisdom among those who are mature, yet not the wisdom of this age, nor of the rulers of this age, who are coming to nothing. But we speak the wisdom of God in a mystery, the hidden wisdom which God ordained before the ages for our glory, which none of the rulers of this age knew; for had they known, they would not have crucified the Lord of Glory. But as it is written: Eye has not seen, nor ear heard, nor have entered into the heart of man the things which God has prepared for those who love Him. But God has revealed them to us through His Spirit. For the Spirit searches all things, yes, the deep things of God."*

And again, Paul reveals this truth in Colossians 1:26–27 and 2:1–4:

> *"The mystery which has been hidden from ages and from generations, but now has been revealed to his saints. To them God willed to make known what are the riches of the glory of this mystery among the Gentiles: which is Christ in you, the hope of glory. . . . For I want you to know what a great conflict I have for you and those in Laodicea, and for as many as have not seen my face in the flesh, that their hearts may be encouraged, being knit together in love, and attaining to all riches of the full assurance of understanding, to the knowledge of the mystery of God, both of the Father and of Christ, in whom are hidden all the treasures of wisdom and knowledge. Now this I say lest anyone should deceive you with persuasive words. For though I am absent in the flesh, yet I am with you in spirit, rejoicing to see your good order and the steadfastness of your faith in Christ."*

The Secret Place

In these verses, Paul speaks of the secret plan and wisdom of God which has been hidden from former generations until now. It is no longer a secret but revealed through the crucifixion and resurrection of Christ. He further states that this mystery is revealed by the Holy Spirit to those who are in Christ Jesus. Relationship—not religion—can only be discovered in your secret place. As we purposefully enter into our prayer closets and spend quality time alone with Him, we cultivate an intimate relationship with Him unlike any we have experienced. (No wonder the devil fights the discipline of prayer so persistently in our lives.)

These are indeed, spiritually speaking, special days we are living in. Through the personal ministry of the Holy Spirit, God is opening our hearts and minds to a deeper revelation of Himself in His Word and prayer. Now, please understand that He is not adding new truth to His written Word. Rather, as Daniel prophesied, our knowledge and understanding of His Word is being illuminated. As we give ourselves to sincere prayer and meditation, Father willingly shares His heart with us in His bedchamber or secret place. And this is not limited to prophets, pastors, teachers, evangelists, or apostles. This gift is available to anyone who seeks Him and is willing to dwell in the secret place.

Understanding that this secret place is in Christ (Colossians 1:27), the obvious question is, How do we find it? In Exodus 33:7–11, we find the answer. Moses had an intimacy with God that few find. We learn from his experience that it's possible to communicate with our Heavenly Father on a personal level.

"Moses took his tent and pitched it outside the camp, far from the camp, and called it the tabernacle of meeting. And it came to pass that

everyone who sought the Lord went out to the tabernacle of meeting which was outside the camp. So it was, whenever Moses went out to the tabernacle, that all the people rose, and each man stood at his tent door and watched Moses until he had gone into the tabernacle. And it came to pass, when Moses entered the tabernacle, that the pillar of cloud descended and stood at the door of the tabernacle, and the Lord talked with Moses. All the people saw the pillar of cloud standing at the tabernacle door, and all the people rose and worshiped, each man in his tent door. So the Lord spoke to Moses face to face, as a man speaks to his friend. and he would return to the camp, but his servant Joshua the son of Nun, a young man, did not depart from the tabernacle."

It is interesting to note how commonly God spoke with Moses. They had an ongoing conversation and Father spoke with him as a friend. I believe this is our Heavenly Father's desire for each of us. However, the major key in understanding the concept of finding and living in this secret place is found in Moses's heart.

What was his motivation? Likewise, we must determine our own motivation in seeking intimacy with God. Unfortunately, many have a false concept of who God is. We view Him as some kind of Robin Hood who takes from the rich and gives to us. We think He exists, simply put, to grant our every desire and to meet our every need. Many even define faith in terms of material possessions and health rather than in relationship with our Heavenly Father.

We look to Him as our provider, protector, and healer, but how many of us know Him as a friend? We are a unique generation that has been taught to seek the hand of God, not His heart.

Before moving on, I encourage you to prayerfully consider

The Secret Place

three requests that Moses made from God in Exodus 33. These requests reveal his heart and the reason why he found such favor with God.

First, in verse 13, he requested that God "show me your intentions" (heart). Above everything else, Moses desired to know God on the same level that his Heavenly Father knew him. He desired intimacy and fellowship with Him.

Second, in verse 15, he requested, "if You don't go with us, personally, don't let us move a step from this place." Moses wanted certainty that he was moving in God's way rather than his own desire. In a true friendship, we always put our friend's needs and desires above our own. We seek to serve the other rather than having them serve us. This was Moses's heart. He refused to take a single step without God's approval.

Third, in verse 18, Moses made his final request: "Let me see Your glory." Moses desired God's presence.

In summarizing these requests, we understand what Moses truly wanted—the heart of God, the will of God, and the presence of God. Prophetically, God placed Moses in the cleft of the rock (Psalm 91), and it was there that He granted Moses his requests. I believe that rock spoke prophetically of Jesus Christ, the rock upon which the Church is built (Matthew 16:18). It is in Christ Jesus, the Rock of Ages, that we find our secret place.

Like Moses, it is in our secret place where we begin to understand the heart of our Heavenly Father. As we intentionally shut out the world and all of its voices, the Holy Spirit has opportunity to impart unto us the very mind of Christ (Philippians 2:7).

It is here that He reveals His secret plan to us and teaches us the value and importance of waiting upon Him. God desires to reveal Himself to us and He delights in fellowship with us just as He did with Moses—face to face as friends.

This level of relationship is only birthed through fellowship. Fellowship with God occurs only in prayer, worship, and meditation. In my next meditation I will share the secret of cultivating intimacy with God through the communion of the Holy Spirit. Our adversary, the devil, once lived in the secret place (in perfect communion with God) and he knows well the personal power and divine influence that comes to those who dwell there.

As we close this first meditation, take a few quiet moments to pray and deeply think about what God has revealed to you here. Ask the Holy Spirit to conduct a screening of your heart and welcome His loving correction as needed. Allow Him to help you in self-evaluation of your motives and attitudes. Bring to the cross whatever He shows you.

A closing thought in preparation for our next meditation: We have so culturized Christianity in America today that many confuse their relationship with God with their relationship with a church or particular denomination. We don't have a relationship with God because we are part of a church. We are in the Church because of our relationship with God. There is a difference. Otherwise, church becomes nothing more than a religious function, a place we attend out of tradition and convenience rather than spiritual conviction.

The world is on a collision course with no hope of survival and tragically, many of us have been blinded by religion. We promote a religious system (the church of man) rather than an intimate, personal relationship with Jesus Christ, who is our hope.

As we prepare to enter into the secret place, prayerfully meditate on this truth.

The Secret Place

In Christ Jesus, Church is not a place we attend,
Nor is it just something we do.
Church is who we are.
Christ in you, the hope of glory!

What a privilege we have to be a part of His Bride, the Church.

MEDITATION 2
Communion of the Holy Spirit

Finally brethren, farewell, become complete. Be of good comfort, be of one mind, live in peace; and the God of love and peace will be with you. Greet one another with a holy kiss. All the saints greet you.

The grace of the Lord Jesus Christ, and the love of God, and the communion of the Holy Spirit be with you all. Amen.

II Corinthians 13:11–14

In his benediction to the Church in Corinth, the Apostle Paul makes a reference to the secret place. This is one of those secrets he referred to in I Corinthians 2:10. Too often we skip over these closing statements as a matter of fact, but it is critically important that we pause and look deeply at what Paul writes. Contained in Paul's words is a mystery that can only be revealed in our prayer closets as we take time to meditate.

The magnitude and significance of what Paul is writing here can only be understood when read as he wrote it, under the inspiration of the Holy Spirit. If we take time to meditate on Scripture, the Holy Spirit who inspired the human authors will illuminate its truth to our hearts and minds.

The Secret Place

Note three key words in verse 14: "The grace of the Lord Jesus Christ, and the Love of God, and the communion of the Holy Spirit be with you all. Amen." The three key words are *grace*, *love*, and *communion*. It is equally important to emphasize the little word *of*. Like all small words used in Scripture, *of* has a depth of meaning. It is a possessive preposition that denotes ownership, belonging to, or coming from. Understanding this, the deep meaning of what Paul is saying comes in focus.

The love we experience as believers comes from and belongs to our Heavenly Father. In mercy, He has extended it to us as a gift that cannot be earned nor deserved.

Likewise, the grace by which you and I have received salvation belongs to the Lord Jesus Christ and has freely been given to us.

Furthermore (and this is the mystery), the communion that we enjoy with God belongs to the Holy Spirit and is given to us out of His deep love for us. Note: the original Greek word for communion that Paul uses here fundamentally means "fellowship." Can you comprehend that God, the Creator of all that exists, desires fellowship (intimacy) with each of us? He does! And through the Holy Spirit, He provides the means to this intimacy. Through the Spirit, God the Father provides the way for us to enter into the veil and fellowship with Him.

Here Paul reveals the heart of our Heavenly Father in a pronounced blessing. Because of His love for us, God sacrificed His son so we could become sons and daughters in His family. Because of the grace of our Lord Jesus Christ, He was willing to become that sacrifice, thus making it possible for us to have a relationship with the Father. And through the personal ministry of the Holy Spirit, we are invited to enter into fellowship with Him. As noted, this communion belongs to the

Holy Spirit, who invites us to partake of the awesome presence of God in our lives. This is relationship, not religion.

To fully comprehend this powerful truth, let me expand on the word *communion*. A very unique word, communion in the original Greek culture of Jesus's day had a very narrow meaning, referencing intimacy. Originally it was used to describe the close relationship between a man and his wife. It is used by the New Testament authors to picture God's desire for a personal and intimate relationship with each of us. A study of the evolution of this word as used in Scripture reveals a spiritual mystery and teaches us the reality of the secret place, where our Father desires to meet us daily.

The New Testament word *bedchamber* is a derivative of the word *communion*. It speaks of a safe place in each home where a husband and wife can openly share their secrets and cultivate a close relationship intended to last forever. In the Jewish home of Jesus's day, this was a room reserved only for parents. Children were taught that this was a sacred place, and they were not permitted to come in unless invited by the Father.

With this understanding, let's go back to our text and see what Paul meant by communion of the Holy Spirit. By using this particular term, Paul communicates that our Heavenly Father, who deeply loves us, has issued a personal invitation to come into His bedchamber, to fellowship with Him in an intimate relationship. This is the reason He calls the Church the Bride of Christ.

He desires one-on-one time with each of us. He invites us into the secret place so He can speak to us face to face as a man speaks to his friend (Exodus 33). This is the most sacred room in our Father's house and, amazingly, He has reserved a room for us.

The Secret Place

> *"Let not your heart be troubled; you believe in God, believe also in Me. In my Father's house are many mansions (bedchambers), if it were not so, I would have told you. I go to prepare a place for you. And if I go and prepare a place for you, I will come again and receive you to Myself; that where I am, there you may be also. And where I go you know, and the way you know." (John 14:1–4)*

It is in the Father's bedchamber that we cultivate a personal relationship with Him. As we linger there, He shares His heart with us. It is also here that the Holy Spirit imparts the very mind of Christ in us (Philippians 2:7). What a revelation for the Last-Day Church! How generous to be given the understanding that God, our Heavenly Father, the Creator of all that exists, the Proprietor of treasures unmeasured, the Alpha and the Omega, the King of Kings, and the Lord of Lords, desires personal fellowship with us. And having been made the Bride of Christ, He invites us into His bedchamber to commune with Him.

With this understanding comes another question we must consider. How do we enter into this sacred place? Note what Jesus said in explaining prayer to us.

> *"And when you pray, you shall not be like the hypocrites. For they love to pray standing in the synagogues and on the corners of the streets, that they may be seen by men. Assuredly, I say to you, they have their reward. But you, when you pray go into your room, and when you have shut the door; pray to your Father who is in the secret place; and your Father who sees in secret will reward you openly. And when you pray, do not use vain repetitions as the heathen do. For they think that they will be heard for their many words." (Matthew 6:5–7)*

Prayer is the door into our Father's bedchamber. This is the only way we can enter into His presence. Here, I must note that the concept of prayer that Jesus taught is much more than what the Church practices. Prayer was never intended by God to be a public demonstration of our spirituality nor a religious formality. Prayer, as taught by Jesus, was a means to have a conversation with your Heavenly Father. It is a very personal experience during which we communicate with Him and He with us. No conversation is complete if it is just one-sided. Conversation is not communication unless both parties have the opportunity to speak and share their feelings and thoughts. So then, prayer is not merely coming to God with a prayer list, but also involves listening to Him.

To be fully functional as God intended, we should understand the different levels of prayer as taught in Scripture.

As we enter into the communion of the Holy Spirit, prayer encompasses every level of communication. It must involve worship, the act of giving honor to God. It also involves praise, our offering of thanksgiving unto the Father for His many blessings. There must be intercession, a time of supplication before God for our needs and the needs of others. It also involves receiving, a time when we listen and receive not only what we desire but, also correction and reproof when needed.

Prayer is made effective by the blood of Jesus Christ. It is through His blood that we gain entrance into the Holy Place and, therefore, prayer should be viewed as an opportunity—not a religious obligation.

Entering into the closet requires time and effort. Our Heavenly Father made it possible to enter into His presence and He has given us a personal invitation to come and stay whenever we desire.

One of the greatest needs in the Church today is

The Secret Place

reprioritizing. We must learn to value personal time with our Lord and intentionally make time to visit His bedchamber on a regular basis. Jesus said "to shut the door and get alone." To obey we have to turn off the TV, radio, computer, and other distractions.

Listening to Christian radio and TV and enjoying Gospel internet programs can be helpful, but we must not let that be our focus. The reason so many never hear the voice of God is because He never has their full attention. Learn to be quiet, to be still and to know that He is God (Psalm 27). You might be surprised at what He shares with you in the secret place.

Struggle to pray? Don't be surprised. The devil constantly fights us in this area. If he can keep us out of the closet he can rob us of God's power, presence, and provision. Determine in your heart and mind right now that you will find your secret place and that you will enter it on a regular basis. Your Father will be pleased, and you will find times of refreshing in His presence.

"Blessed are they which do hunger and thirst after righteousness: for they shall be filled." (Matthew 5:6)

MEDITATION 3
THE DIFFICULTY OF PRAYER

"And when thou prayest, thou shalt not be as the hypocrites are: for they love to pray standing in the synagogues and in the corners of the streets, that they may be seen of men. Verily I say unto you, they have their reward. But thou, when thou prayest, enter into thy closet, and when thou hast shut thy door, pray to thy Father which is in the secret place; and thy Father which seeth in secret shall reward thee openly."

—Matthew 6:5–6

We closed our previous meditation noting that prayer is the doorway into the secret place. As I write this meditation, Jane and I are at home like the entire nation, quarantined due to the horrific COVID-19 virus. This morning we are also experiencing severe weather and have been placed under a tornado warning. These are indeed critical times in which we are living and all over the world we see what I call forced prayer. That's not a negative. It's just reality. People who seldom pray are taking time to seek God, asking for His protection and provision. Because of these difficult times and

The Secret Place

the timely revelation of the secret place truth, this meditation addresses spiritual warfare.

Knowing that prayer is the doorway into our Father's presence (bedchamber) and that Biblical prayer is a conversation with God, we should not be surprised that developing a consistent and effective prayer life is one of the greatest battles we will face. Satan knows the power of prayer and will do anything to keep us out of our prayer closets.

Note the priority and purpose that the Apostle James gives to prayer in the fifth chapter of his Epistle (James 5:16).

"Confess your trespasses to one another, and pray for one another, that you may be healed. The effective, fervent prayer of a righteous man avails much."

If we truly believe this, why do we have such a difficult time with the discipline of prayer? If prayer is the door into our Father's presence and provision, it stands to reason that we would value and enjoy our prayer times. However, praying fervently (with passion) on a daily basis is an ongoing battle that too often we lose. There are so many distractions to stop us, and when we do find the time to pray, we are often too tired to properly focus.

Satan understands the power released in personal prayer. He is a master at distracting and preventing us from entering into our prayer closets (war rooms). Prayer is one of the most powerful weapons that God has given us and if we are going to overcome our enemy, we must heed James's admonition and make prayer a high priority in our lives.

One of the most touching scenes in the Bible is recorded in each of the four Gospels. We are taken with Jesus into the

Garden of Gethsemane with His disciples. At this point in the Gospels, the disciples have been with Jesus for more than three years, hearing Him teach and experiencing many miracles.

They know He is the Messiah, the son of God. The night before His crucifixion, Jesus faces the most critical hour of His earthly life. He was struggling and He asked the disciples to hold Him up in prayer. Their response? Falling asleep. Twice He comes to them and twice they go to sleep.

I believe this is a prophetic picture of the Last-Day Church, in which we participate today. The disciples could not pray with their Master and Lord for a single hour. How many of us do the same? We come to church and sing with great joy and energy. We plan a fellowship meal and every seat is taken. Plan a prayer meeting, however, and the room is nearly empty.

Most churches have stopped calling Wednesday night "prayer meetings," because they aren't. And pastors don't want to lie. If we desire to participate in the Army of God in these critical times, we must become prayer warriors. Winning soldiers don't wait until the battle starts to prepare for warfare. They train endlessly to be prepared when the battle begins. In the Church we must develop this same mentality. We must prioritize prayer and reinvent the prayer meeting on personal and congregational levels.

In history, every revival and great move of God was birthed in prayer. The great revivals of the Wesleys, Charles Finney, and the Azusa Street outpouring from the early 1900s all came to fruition through fervent prayer. The same truth remains today.

Effective, fervent prayer is birthed in understanding prayer as taught in Scripture. Prayer is not a religious rite. Nor is it just a means of receiving blessings from our Heavenly Father. It is communication with God and is birthed in relationship,

The Secret Place

not religion. Jesus taught about prayer in many places, including Matthew 7:7–8.

> *"Ask and it will be given to you; seek, and you will find; knock, and it will be opened to you. For everyone who asks receives, and he who seeks will find, and to him who knocks it will be opened."*

Here we learn that there are three levels of praying. To pray right, we must discern which level is required. Asking occurs when we clearly know the will of God as revealed in His word by the Holy Spirit. It is not just randomly speaking what we want (our will) but rather asking for what we understand to be God's will and purpose. When we know the will of God, He delights in meeting even our desires, because our desires will be changed to match his (Psalm 37). The second level is seeking. This occurs in circumstances where we do not know what Father wants in a particular situation. And the third level is knocking, the focus of this meditation.

We're led to knock when the Holy Spirit opens our eyes to the mind and will of God in a situation. Knocking involves intercessory prayer, during which we use the knowledge that the Spirit gives and ask that God's will be done, His kingdom come.

A great example of knocking is found in Daniel 10. God gives Daniel a vision, which Daniel understands but he does not know when the vision will become reality. He purposes in his heart to pray (knock) and fast until it comes. For twenty-one days he fasts and prays (the basis of the Daniel Fast) until an angel appears and explains why he was so long in coming to Daniel:

> *"Then he said to me, 'Do not fear, Daniel, for from the first day*

that you set your heart to understand, and to humble yourself before your God, your words were heard; and I have come because of your words. But the prince of the kingdom of Persia (a demon spirit) withstood me twenty-one days; and behold, Michael, one of the chief princes (angels), came to help me, for I had been left alone there with the kings of Persia.'" (Daniel 10:12–13—parentheses mine)

Daniel was persistent in knocking until he received his answer. From the first day he prayed, God heard and responded, but the angel bringing his answer was withstood in the heavenly places for twenty-one days—hence the need for spiritual armor, as described in Ephesians 6:10. It was only after assistance came from Michael the Chief Angel that the answer could be delivered.

This is the same spiritual warfare we are involved in. It is critical that we understand this and become equally determined in our prayer efforts. Knocking is not easy and requires spiritual patience and strength. Prayer is work, and in the midst of spiritual warfare, it can be hard work.

Note this exhortation from James.

"Therefore submit to God. Resist the devil and he will flee from you. Draw near to God and He will draw near to you. Cleanse your hands, you sinners; and purify your hearts, you double-minded. Lament and mourn and weep! Let your laughter be turned to mourning and your joy to gloom. Humble yourselves in the sight of the Lord, and He will lift you up." (James 4:7–10)

Drawing near to God requires effort. We must intentionally come and sincerely allow Him to search our hearts and through the work of His Holy Spirit to cleanse us of any attitude or activity not pleasing to Him. This is not a comfortable process, but note the results: "He will draw near us . . . ." If we do our part, God will do His. If we listen, He will speak.

Let me expand on this by sharing the three Ds of a defeated prayer life, which identify three enemy strategies we battle on an ongoing basis. It is imperative that we recognize and overcome these in our prayer efforts. These three defeaters are distress, depression, and distraction.

Distress is one of the most complicated and horrendous tools that Satan uses to keep us out of our prayer closet. How we deal with it will determine how deeply we grow into the image of Christ. Distress manifests itself in our daily lives through worry, anxiety, frustration, and stress. Satan's main interest in producing distress is to rob us of the presence, peace, and provision of our Heavenly Father.

As you've likely noticed, it's not difficult to get people to pray when they are confronted with distress. However, it is another matter to get them to pray rightly (effectively).

Too often when we are attacked with distress, the distress becomes our total focus, and our prayer time is turned into a pity party during which we murmur, complain, and even blame God for our difficulties. Prayer should never be used to complain ("Do all things without murmurings"—Philippians 2:14), but rather as a vehicle into the very presence of God where we discover deliverance, healing, and comfort.

In Psalm 100 we are instructed to enter into His presence with thanksgiving.

> *"Make a joyful shout to the lord, all you lands!*
> *Serve the LORD with gladness;*

Come before his presence with singing.
Know that the LORD, He is God;
It is He who has made us, and not we ourselves;
We are His people and the sheep of His pasture.
Enter into His gates with thanksgiving,
And into His courts with praise.
Be thankful to Him, and bless His name.
For the LORD is good; His mercy is everlasting,
And His truth endures to all generations."

When we obey this principle and enter into His presence with a heart of gratitude, even if we don't feel like it, we are acknowledging His sovereignty over our lives. This powerfully defeats the devil's attempt to crush our spirit and blind us to God's blessings. When we praise God when things are difficult and/or painful, we exalt Him as Lord. This is what the author of Hebrews refers to as a sacrifice of praise (13:15): "Therefore by Him let us continually offer the sacrifice of praise to God, that is, the fruit of our lips, giving thanks to His name."

The same truth is taught in Psalm 149:5–6:

"Let the saints be joyful in glory; let them sing aloud on their beds. Let the high praises of God be in their mouth, and a two-edged sword in their hand."

The sacrifice of praise and the high praises refer to praising God in difficulty, through faith. When we look beyond our circumstances and give God the praise that He deserves, in spite of how we feel or don't feel, we give Him glory and not our enemy. Herein lies the power of praise and the priority of fervent prayer. Jesus said as long as we are in this world we will

The Secret Place

have tribulations. But He instructs us to rejoice because He has overcome the world. To acknowledge this we must learn, as Paul taught us, to give thanks in every situation.

"In everything give thanks; for this is the will of God in Christ Jesus concerning you." (I Thessalonians 5:18)

In doing this, we give God the glory by allowing ourselves to be governed by our faith, not our feelings. Be reminded that you are never alone. Your Heavenly Father knows and sees every circumstance and situation of your life and He is bigger than any problem you have. There is not a disease that He cannot heal nor a problem that He can't solve.

He and He alone is our Peace-giver, our Protector, and our Provider. If you tuck this truth in your heart and mind, distress will never conquer you—even in the midst of disease, famine, or death. Praise in prayer brings you into God's wonderful presence and it is in His presence that you will find fullness of joy.

"You will show me the path of life; in your presence is fullness of joy; at your right hand are pleasures forevermore." (Psalm 16:11)

In His presence, distress cannot massacre your emotions. Nor can it defeat your faith by quenching the flame of hope that burns in your heart. To further stress this, listen carefully to what the Holy Spirit spoke through Paul in Philippians 4:6. "Be anxious for nothing, but in everything by prayer and supplication, with thanksgiving, let your request be known to God." Even if your healing doesn't come this side of eternity, He is still God and still provides strength to move forward without fear or worry.

With this powerful truth in mind, determine that you will conquer all the distress in your life through prayer rather than allowing distress to keep you out of your secret place. Prayer may not always change the circumstances in your life, but quality time spent in your secret place will certainly change your perception of them. In Christ Jesus, we are victors not victims (Romans 8:37).

Please understand that the heart of the battle is not in the circumstances of your life but more powerfully in your mind. Before moving to the second D, let me restate an all-important truth. There is nothing that will drive away the spirit of distress in your life quicker than an attitude of gratitude: "Giving thanks always for all things unto God and the Father in the name of our Lord Jesus Christ." (Ephesians 5:20)

The second defeater of prayer is the often overwhelming spirit of depression. Please note that I refer to depression as a "spirit" and not just a sickness or mental illness. Although it certainly has the ability to make one sick and many who are confronted with this dilemma over a long period of time become mentally challenged, it is basically a spiritual force from the pits of hell. As such, depression is one of the most common and powerful weapons Satan has devised to conquer the people of God. As stated earlier, it is a mind battle. When ignored, neglected, or accepted, it has the capability of rendering its victims totally ineffective in every area of life.

You might be surprised to learn that many of the most successful men and women of God have personally fought this demon. If you study closely the lives and ministry of our heroes of faith named in God's Hall of Fame in Hebrews 11, you will discover that many of them faced this formidable foe. Moses became so discouraged under its influence that he actually prayed for God to kill him. Elijah, the Prophet, who prayed down the fire of God and brought an entire nation to its knees,

The Secret Place

sat under a juniper tree and cried that God would kill him and let him go.

Additionally, in my study of Church history, I have learned that some of the greatest preachers who have ever occupied the pulpit at times have revealed their battle with this spirit. They testify of being so depressed at times that they could not function. Like them, this devastating enemy can render you helpless, hopeless, and in a state of mind that forbids you from seeing the greatness and goodness of your Heavenly Father, who loves you dearly.

Depression creates an all-consuming feeling of aloneness that seeks to isolate you emotionally and physically. If not resisted, it will cause you to believe that no one loves you or cares how you feel, especially God and close friends and family. It can create in you an overwhelming sense of disconnectedness, rendering you unable to function, let alone fight it. When it is permitted to run its course in your life, it will have a profound effect on your physical, emotional, and spiritual health. It alters reality in your thinking and causes you to see and hear things differently than what they are. It robs you of motivation and keeps you in a state of despair to the point that you become emotionally paralyzed.

Before you panic, let me state emphatically that depression can be defeated. Contrary to what the enemy and others may have convinced you of, with God's help you can win this battle. I write out of my own experience.

The first step to overcoming this spirit is to acknowledge its hold on you, to admit that you need help. And you are not alone in this battle. Please understand that suffering from depression doesn't mean that you have failed God or that you've sinned. It doesn't mean that you don't have faith, but if not dealt with, it can destroy your faith and hope. It is important to know that just because you are depressed now doesn't mean you always will be. Don't let anyone or anything convince you that you cannot overcome this ugly spirit.

During my five decades of pastoral ministry, I've witnessed many good and precious believers be destroyed by this foe, having been made to believe that there was no hope of recovery. The devil is the father of lies!

Too many turn to mind-altering drugs or alcohol for relief. I'm not suggesting that taking medication is wrong, but at best it only deals with the symptoms. Jesus heals and delivers. I have seen some of the most precious people in the Kingdom totally destroyed by becoming addicted to opioids and other prescription drugs.

Unfortunately, some counselors and doctors are quick to write a prescription simply because it's the easiest thing to do and many don't believe there is a cure, only treatment. Out of this thinking we have created a drug-dependent society that lives in dysfunction.

It is not my intention to put anyone under guilt or condemnation. I write out of sincere compassion and deep concern for God's people who are dealing with this horrific force. Satan wants to convince you that there is no hope, but he is wrong. God loves you and will set you free. And "whom the Son sets free is free indeed."

Because depression comes from a spirit, it must be dealt with through the Spirit of God. Once you acknowledge that it is a problem in your life, then you can openly deal with it by seeking God's help. This brings us back to prayer.

Prayer is a powerful weapon God has given to us to combat the enemy on every front. I believe that in the battle against

The Secret Place

depression and every other disease, disorder, trial, or tribulation, prayer is the most effective tool we have. God often uses medication as a means to bring healing, but Jesus is the healer, who heals and delivers by destroying the root cause.

Note what David wrote in Psalm 46:

> *"God is our refuge and strength,*
> *A very present help in trouble.*
> *Therefore we will not fear,*
> *Even though the earth be removed,*
> *And though the mountains be carried into the midst of the sea."*

Prayer is the doorway into our Father's secret place, and it is there where we find refuge from our enemies and Satan's schemes against us.

In the Father's house, the Holy Spirit illuminates the truth of God's Word to our hearts and minds. It's here that we discover who we are and the power and authority that has been imparted to us in Jesus's name. With this understanding of who we are in Christ, we have the power to bind the horrific spirit of depression and its effect upon us. Depression is centered in our emotions (feelings), and the only thing that can change how we feel is the all-powerful presence of God in our lives.

Note the declarations of the Psalmist:

> *"For you have made him most blessed forever; you have made him exceedingly glad with your presence." (21:6)*
> *"You are my hiding place; you shall preserve me from trouble; you shall surround me with songs of deliverance." (32:3)*
> *"The angel of the Lord encamps all around those who fear him, and delivers them." (34:7)*

As we commune with our Heavenly Father, we enter into His presence, where depression has no option but to loosen its grip on us and exit. Again, this is why a consistent, disciplined prayer life is so vitally important for each of us. It has little or nothing to do with how we feel; we pray in faith and not in human feelings. God is God whether we feel Him or not. He is working even when we can't see it. Our circumstances do not change who God is, but in praise and prayer, God can and will change our circumstances.

Before we move to the final D, meditate on this truth: Faith not feeling conquers depression. Otherwise, depression defeats our faith and destroys our feelings.

The third and final D in the battle of prayer is distraction. This is the most seductive tool that Satan has devised to undermine prayer. Distraction is particularly dangerous because it is socially acceptable. Unlike distress and depression, distraction is easily overlooked. Few realize they're being distracted or feel distraction is a bad thing.

Many believers find it difficult to maintain an intimate relationship with their Heavenly Father simply because they are consistently distracted by less important things. It's not because they don't want to pray or don't sense the need to pray. Rather, they can't find time to pray on a regular basis. It is a silent killer that sneaks in to destroy and we fail to recognize it because it is socially acceptable.

Sadly, when you find time to spend with the Father, you fall asleep out of fatigue or a lack of energy, just as Jesus's original disciples. And most often, we argue that the things we busy ourselves with are both good and necessary—things for family and Church. However, even good things can be abused and misused, changed from useful ways to grow God's kingdom to worldly burdens. Too many of God's people have fallen into this trap. We are so busy that we have little time or energy for true communion with our Heavenly Father. He grieves our absence and longs for fellowship with us but we're not available.

It is unthinkable that we could miss a day at work or that our kids could miss a practice or ballgame, yet we think little about missing a church service and even less about not praying on a regular basis. The truth of the matter is today we have plenty of time to play but no time to pray.

The painful reality is that many believers are committing spiritual adultery and don't even realize it. Like David, we need a Nathan to wake us up. Regardless of how busy your life may be, finding time to pray is never a matter of time. It is a question of priority. We have become so distracted by the blessings in life that we have lost touch with the Blesser. What is even more tragic is that many in ministry are so busy in the Church that we lose touch with Him.

In Luke 2, we're given a prophetic picture of the Last-Day Church that I will share in a forthcoming meditation, but let me insert this present-day reality. The Christian faith is now found more places around the planet than at any other time. There is Christian broadcasting twenty-four hours a day via TV, radio, and internet. There are thousands of local churches, denominational and independent, proclaiming the Gospel in every community. We could attend a church function every day of the week if we so desired.

Despite the prevalence of churches and Christianity, the world is falling apart. Crime is uncontrollable. Abortions are everyday occurrences. Addiction to alcohol and drugs is a global epidemic. One out of three marriages ends in divorce. One of every five kids struggle with emotional or mental illness.

How can this be with a church on every street corner?

We can sanctuary ourselves in our million-dollar facilities and blame the government, society, and everybody else, but the stark reality is that the Church is failing. We have religion but not relationship with the living God. We faithfully attend Church services, where worship has been turned into a science. We know the right words and when to sit and stand. We know our church's specific theology and emphasis. We know how to dress and not to dress. But do we know God? Like Mary and Joseph, we celebrate our religious high days, but on the way home, we discover that we have lost Jesus.

With religion, we can go through all the functions, but a fervent relationship with God requires daily prayer. Consistent, disciplined, and effective praying conquers all distress, depression, and distraction in your life (Romans 8), because it puts our focus not on ourselves but on our Heavenly Father. In Christ we are more than conquerors and prayer cultivates intimacy with your Heavenly Father and brings you into His bedchamber (secret place). It is only there, in communion with the Holy Spirit, that He is able to share His heart with us. It is there that we receive understanding and revelation as to who and where we are in life.

No wonder Paul instructs us to pray without ceasing (I Thessalonians 5:17). He is not suggesting that we stay in prayer twenty-four hours a day, but that we always walk in the Spirit with a sense of God's presence in our lives. We should never be in a position or place where God cannot speak to us. This is what the Psalmist meant when he said "to dwell in the secret place." Only through Jesus Christ is that possible, and we must intentionally seek Him to dwell there.

MEDITATION 4
UNDERSTANDING OUR TIMES

Knowing this first, that there shall come in the last days scoffers, walking after their own lusts, and saying, where is the promise of his coming? For since the fathers fell asleep, all things continue as they were from the beginning of the creation. For this they willingly are ignorant of, that by the word of God the heavens were of old, and the earth standing out of the water and in the water: whereby the world that then was, being overflowed with water, perished. But the heavens and the earth, which are now, by the same word are kept in store, reserved unto fire against the day of judgment and perdition of ungodly men. But, beloved, be not ignorant of this one thing, that one day is with the Lord as a thousand years, and a thousand years as one day. The Lord is not slack concerning His promise, as some men count slackness; but is longsuffering to us-ward, not willing that any should perish, but that all should come to repentance. But the day of the Lord will come as a thief in the night; in which the heavens shall pass away with a great noise, and the elements shall melt with fervent heat, the earth also and the works that are therein shall be burned up.

II Peter 3: 3–10

The Secret Place

Up to this point our focus has been exclusively on how we can cultivate a personal and intimate relationship with our Heavenly Father through the grace of the Lord Jesus Christ and communion with the Holy Spirit. In our final meditations, I will direct our attention to the all-important subject of the last days and where we are in God's timeline for all ages.

As we embark on this journey, let me assure you that it is not my intention to speculate on the specific day or time of Christ's return. Scripture is very clear that no man knows that day. However, Jesus did teach us that we should know the season in which He would return:

> *"But of that day and hour no one knows, not even the angels of Heaven, but my Father only. But as the days of Noah were, so also will the coming of the Son of Man be." (Matthew 24:36–37)*

Ezekiel's prophecy, recorded in the Old Testament, is just as relevant today as it was when he received it in 593 BC. Much of what he saw in the Spirit and wrote in the last fifteen chapters of his book is unfolding today before our very own eyes. Today, the prophetic voice of God is being heard by those who have "ears to hear and eyes to see." We are being comforted, convicted, and corrected by the truths that Father is making known unto us. How interesting that God, through His prophets, reveals His plans to us.

On one hand, we are disturbed by current events happening around us that cause us to understand that the Age of the Gentiles is quickly coming to an end.

> *"And they will fall by the edge of the sword, and be led away*

captive into all nations. And Jerusalem will be trampled by Gentiles until the times of the Gentiles are fulfilled." (Luke 21:24)

However, on the other hand, there is great spiritual excitement and anticipation being birthed in our hearts as we realize Jesus will soon return for His bride, the Church. It is this same excitement that caused the Apostle Paul to keep his eyes heavenward when the weight of Earth threatened to crush him.

"For I consider that the sufferings of this present time are not worthy to be compared with the glory which shall be revealed in us. For the earnest expectation of the creation eagerly awaits for the revealing of the sons of God. For the creation was subject to futility, not willingly, but because of Him who subjected it in hope; because the creation itself also will be delivered from the bondage of corruption into the glorious liberty of the children of God. For we know that the whole creation groans and labors with birth pangs together until now." (Romans 8:18–22)

Our Heavenly Father delights in revealing His plans for the ages to those who take time to dwell in the secret place. As we enter into His presence and wait upon Him, God shares His secrets to us by the Holy Spirit (re-read I Corinthians 2:6–10). He is not only revealing His plan to adopt those who turn to Him for salvation, but He is also showing us the season in which we are now living. During His earthly ministry, Jesus clearly taught prophetically concerning the days in which we now live.

"Now learn this parable from the fig tree: when its branch has already become tender and puts forth leaves, you know that summer is near. So, you also, when you see all these things, know that it is near

The Secret Place

at the doors! Assuredly, I say to you, this generation will by no means pass away till all these things take place. Heaven and earth will pass away, but my words will by no means pass away." (Matthew 24: 32–35)

Furthermore, He issued this warning:

"But take heed to yourselves, lest your hearts be weighed down with carousing, drunkenness, and cares of this life, and that day come on you unexpectedly. For it will come as a snare on all those who dwell on the face of the whole earth. Watch therefore, and pray always that you may be counted worthy to escape all these things that will come to pass, and to stand before the Son of Man." (Luke 21:34–36)

The Father controls the appointed hour and our responsibility, as believers, is to discern the times and to warn our generation (as Noah did) that He is indeed coming back for those who look for Him. "So Christ was offered once to bear the sins of many. To those who eagerly wait for Him He will appear a second time, apart from sin, for salvation." (Hebrews 9:28)

I encourage you to pause and think deeply of our concept and understanding of time. Truthfully, our experience of time is one thing we all have in common. It doesn't matter how educated we are, how much money we have, or what echelon of society we live in, we are each bound to a certain timeline.

How we manage the time that we have been given determines the quality of life we have. Those who master their use of time find success and those who abuse it never have enough of it. And lost time can never be recovered. Once an hour has passed, it is forever gone.

All of us, at some point, take time for granted, yet every day and in every area of our lives, time has the final say. I learned early in my ministry that it didn't matter how busy I was or what I gave my attention to, Sunday would always come, and I had to be prepared. Likewise, it is critically important to understand just how limited time is. Additionally, we should sincerely ask our Heavenly Father to show us His understanding of this precious commodity He has given us.

Scripture clearly teaches that God created time and set everything in motion at the beginning of His Creation.

"Then God said, 'Let there be light;' and there was light. And God saw the light, that it was good; and God divided the light from the darkness. God called the light day, and the darkness he called night. So the evening and the morning were the first day." (Genesis 1: 3–6)

To fully understand God's established timeline we must acknowledge that His concept of time differs from ours. We measure everything by a set calendar and a standardized time table. However, God is omnipresent and is not confined to time as we are. He has revealed Himself to us as the beginning and the end: "I am the Alpha and the Omega, the beginning and the end, says the Lord, who is and who was and who is to come, the Almighty." (Revelation 1:8)

In reality, God is timeless in both nature and person. He has no yesterdays nor tomorrows. He has and always will be a "now" God. "Jesus Christ is the same yesterday, today, and forever." (Hebrews 13:8) He is unchangeable and timeless, always existing in the present. There never has been a time when God did not exist and there will never be a time when He ceases to be.

"God is spirit, and those who worship Him must worship

The Secret Place

in spirit and truth." (John 4:24) Because He is spirit, God is not confined to time and space as we are. Our difficulty comprehending this is due to our perception. We want God to come down in our time to reveal Himself to us—as He did 2,000 years ago—but what He desires is to lift us up by His Spirit and give us a revelation of Himself, in His time. Note what the Apostle Paul wrote to the Ephesian believers.

> *"Blessed be the God and Father of our Lord Jesus Christ, who hath blessed us with every spiritual blessing in the heavenly places in Christ." (Ephesians 1:3)*

Both Paul and John were taken by the Spirit into the third heaven. It is His desire to show each of us His plans. Even though God, Himself, is timeless, He has by an act of His own will established a divine timeline in creation that involves you and me. According to Paul in Ephesians 1:4, this plan began before the foundation of the world and continues until today. This timeline is a very important part of God's plan, from the very beginning until now.

> *"He is the image of the invisible God, the firstborn over all creation. For by Him all things were created that are in Heaven and that are on the earth, visible and invisible, whether thrones or dominions or principalities or powers. All things were created through Him and for Him. And He is before all things, and in Him all things consist. And He is the head of the body, the Church, who is the beginning, the firstborn from the dead, that in all things He may have the preeminence." (Colossians 1:15–18)*

Our understanding of this plan (timeline) is essential to

understanding the times in which we live and the strategic role that each of us play. In II Peter 3:8, the Apostle Peter writes "that with the Lord one day is as a thousand years, and a thousand years as one day." This reveals several important truths to us. First, God's concept of time is different from ours. Second, God has an established timeline for the Ages. And third, God is a God of divine order who does nothing by coincidence or chance. Rather, everything He has done and will do is in accordance with His plan.

Sincerely, in my heart and mind, I do not know when our Lord will return for us. But in my spirit, I believe something phenomenal is just around the corner. We are truly a chosen generation and it is time to get serious about our walk with God. We need to ask ourselves some deep and probing questions. Could this really be the midnight hour into which our Lord will return as a thief in the night?

"But the day of the Lord will come as a thief in the night, in which the heavens will pass away with a great noise, and the elements will melt with fervent heat; both the earth and the works that are in it will be burned up." (II Peter 3:10)

Could this really be the end of the Gentile age spoken of by Jesus in Luke 21:24? Is life as we know it quickly coming to an end? Prayerfully consider and meditate on what John wrote in his first Epistle:

"Do not love the world or the things in the world. If anyone loves the world, the love of the Father is not in him. For all that is in the world—the lust of the flesh, the lust of the eyes, and the pride of life—is not of the Father but is of the world. And the world is

THE SECRET PLACE

passing away, and the lust of it; but he who does the will of God abides forever. Little children, it is the last hour; and as you have heard that the Antichrist is coming, even now many Antichrists have come, by which we know it is the last hour." (I John 1:15–18)

MEDITATION 5
SIGNS OF THE TIMES

"But of that day and hour no one knows, not even the angels of heaven, but my Father only. But as the days of Noah were, so also will the coming of the Son of Man be. For as in the day before the flood, they were eating and drinking, marrying and giving in marriage, until the day that Noah entered the ark, and did not know until the flood came and took them all away, so also will the coming of the Son of Man be. Then two men will be in the field: one will be taken and the other left. Two women will be grinding at the mill: one will be taken and the other left. Watch therefore, for you do not know what hour your Lord is coming. But know this, that if the master of the house had known what hour the thief would come, he would have watched and not allowed his house to be broken into. Therefore you also be ready, for the Son of Man is coming at an hour you do not expect."

Matthew 24:36–44

In a lengthy discourse recorded in Matthew 24 and Luke 21, Jesus—in response to His disciples' questions—gives an in-depth look at the last generation, the End-Time Church. A close examination of these texts reveal that Jesus's intent

The Secret Place

was not to discuss the end-time events, but rather, the disciples' need to understand true discipleship. It is interesting to note that these "revelation" chapters are prophetic in their structure as well as content. To fully understand the context of what Jesus says here, we need to note the time and setting in which it was stated.

Jesus and His disciples are at a service in the local synagogue, as their custom was. When the offering was received, Jesus found an opportunity to teach the disciples (and us) a valuable lesson regarding what true worship and service to God really is.

> *"And He looked up and saw the rich putting their gifts into the treasury, and He saw also a certain poor widow putting in two mites. So He said, 'Truly I say to you that this poor widow has put in more than all; for all these out of their abundance have put in offerings for God, but she out of her poverty put in all the livelihood that she had.'"* (Luke 21:1–4)

However, note that in verses 5–6, the disciples did not even acknowledge Jesus's observation or what He was saying.

> *"Then, as some spoke of the temple, how it was adorned with beautiful stones and donations, He said, 'These things which you see—the days will come in which not one stone shall be left upon another that shall not be thrown down . . .'"*

The disciples' focus was on the beautiful building, the memorial stones, and the marvelous works that the people had built. They read carefully each name plate on the wall that revealed what each person had given, and they were amazed at the works of man.

Unfortunately, many are like the early disciples, who view things from the human perspective and have deaf ears to what God is teaching. He speaks, but are we really listening? We have culturized Christianity to fit into our mold rather than seeking our Father's purpose and plan. Many are content serving God out of convenience rather than conviction. Our culture teaches us to hear without listening, and we have been excellent students. There is noise everywhere we go. Whether at work, restaurants, shopping stores, or in our cars, something is always playing in the background. To hear the Holy Spirit, we must be intentional. This is why He closes His message to each Church in Revelation (the End-Time Church) with this exhortation:

"He who has an ear, let him hear what the Spirit says to the churches. To him who overcomes I will give to eat from the tree of life, which is in the midst of the paradise of God." (Revelation 2:7)

In Luke 21 when Jesus realized the disciples were not paying attention, He changed the subject with a statement (prophecy) that got the disciples' full attention. He spoke of a designated time to come in which life as they knew it would end and the things that they admired would be utterly destroyed. Wow! He knew just how to get their attention.

I believe our Heavenly Father is doing the same thing today. We are seeing cataclysmic changes in our world. Many of these unprecedented events are prophesied in Scriptures and some interpret them as the judgment of God upon a people who have forsaken Him. Certainly, this could be true. But it could also be the grace of God trying to get our attention before it is too late.

The Secret Place

Much of what Jesus taught in Matthew 24 and Luke 21 is unfolding before our very eyes. I just have to wonder how far He will have to go before He has our full attention. At some point, as prophesied, His patience will run out and things will end just as He spoke. I do not know when that time is but He warns us that it will come unexpectedly, as a thief in the night. Only those who have developed ears to hear and eyes to see will know it.

As learned previously, God's concept of time differs from ours. Understanding His timeline helps us to know that we are now living in that season. God is in the process of completing His plan for all the ages and life as we know it will soon end. We do not know the specific day or hour that this will take place, but in Matthew 24 and Luke 21, Jesus clearly teaches that we should know the season and revealed four specific signs to help us do just that.

Before cataloging these four signs, let me address a question I often hear regarding the last days: When did the last days actually begin?

Our answer is found in Hebrews 1:1–2.

"God who at various times and in various ways spoke in times past to the fathers by the prophets, has in these last days spoken to us by his Son, whom He has appointed heir of all things, through whom also He made the worlds."

According to these verses, the last days of God's timeline began with the birth of Jesus in Bethlehem. Christ's birth (incarnation) and the subsequent birth of the Church on the Day of Pentecost in Acts 2 was the beginning of what Scripture teaches to be the Age of the Gentiles.

> *"And they will fall by the edge of the sword, and be led away captive into all nations. And Jerusalem will be trampled by Gentiles until the times of the Gentiles are fulfilled." (Luke 21:24)*

We are clearly taught that this current age in which we now live will come to a sudden end by the appearing of Christ (the rapture) to be reunited with His bride,[1] the Church. This phenomenal event will throw the world into a period of seven years of tribulation. At the conclusion of those already appointed days, Christ will return to the earth for one thousand years, a period known as the millennium. At the end of this, there will be a cataclysmic war in which everything will be destroyed, thus starting a new era and the completion of God's eternal plan. New heavens and a new earth will appear and the kingdom of God will be established forever.

I am convinced that you and I are privileged to be alive in this historical moment. It is clear to all who seriously study His Word that we are now in preparation for this climatic change. The next prophecy to be fulfilled is the rapture of His Church.

> *"And I heard, as it were, the voice of a great multitude, as the sound of many waters and as the sound of mighty thunderings, saying, 'Alleluia! For the Lord God omnipotent reigns! Let us be glad and rejoice and give him glory, for the marriage of the lamb has come, and his wife has made herself ready.' And to her it was granted to be arrayed in fine linen, clean and bright, for the fine linen is the righteous acts of the saints." (Revelation 19:6–8)*

The four specific signs that Jesus spoke of in Matthew 24 and Luke 21 were to take place right before the rapture of the

The Secret Place

Church and the seven-year period of tribulation. He shared them with us so that we would know the season and that we could prepare by living in a state of readiness for His return. Too much is happening for us to simply look at these events as being futuristic. Rather, we must understand that prophecy is being fulfilled daily as proposed and planned by God.

The first of these signs focus on God's chosen people, Israel. Our Jewish brothers and sisters are special to our Heavenly Father because He chose them to be the original recipients of His eternal covenant. It was out of their seed that our Messiah would be born. During His earthly ministry, Jesus prophesied confirming the many prophecies of the Old Testament, that Israel would be center stage of the entire world, in the last days. They were destined to play a strategic role in the last days.

No one who is informed on current events, can deny that these prophecies are currently being fulfilled. This small Middle-Eastern region occupies more space in the news than any other subject. All eyes are upon Israel and the Palestinian area. Endless peace talks and billions of dollars are earmarked towards them, hoping for peace and stability. Yet, Jesus and the prophets taught that when all attention was on peace, sudden destruction would surely come. The world sits in anticipation of a Mid-East peace treaty, but it will not happen until the Prince of Peace appears. This is why we are instructed in Scripture to pray for the peace of Jerusalem.

Not only is the secular community focused on Israel, but Israel has captured the Christian Church's interest over the last two decades as well. We look to Israel to gain understanding of prophecy so we can clearly hear what the Spirit is saying to us in this critical hour.

I recently had the awesome experience of visiting the Holy

Land on a tour led by a dear friend of mine, Rabbi Paul Klassen, a Messianic Jewish believer, and two well-informed Israeli historians who are citizens there. It was a life-changing ten days for me and the forty from our church who were privileged to attend. Biblical history came alive as we traced the footsteps of Jesus and viewed the locations of His life and ministry. Thousands of years of Bible stories were relived and all of us returned home with a deep conviction and confirmation of our faith.

Through His Covenant with Israel, God reveals His unfailing love for the human family. By His ultimate sacrifice on the cross, Jesus as the Lamb of God made it possible for you and me to be spiritually born into the Jewish family and thus be partakers of all of God's promised blessings. Therefore, their history is our history, and through the blood of Christ, their covenant has become our covenant. Everything in this covenant points to the return of our Messiah for His bride, the Church.

The second sign taught in the Gospels is focused on the Church and her prophetic role in the last days. Jesus taught of three (prophetic number) signs that would be evident in the Last-Day Church.

First, He warned that the Church would be inundated with false prophets and teachers who would try to change the truth of God into a lie, convincing people to serve the creature (themselves) not the Creator (God). He stated that some would even claim to be the Christ. Note that it does not say they would claim to be Jesus but the Christ, the way to salvation. Sadly, any church denomination or religious group who teaches that the way into Heaven is through their specific teachings is fulfilling this sign. Jesus is the only way into eternal life.

The Secret Place

Another part of this second sign is found in the nature and climate found in the Last-Day Church. There would be two things happening within the Church at the same time. It has been prophesied that in the last days a great falling away would happen with many believers turning away from God and His Church being deceived (seduced) by doctrines of devils.

"Now the Spirit expressly says that in latter times some will depart from the faith, giving heed to deceiving spirits and doctrines of demons, speaking lies in hypocrisy, having their own conscience seared with a hot iron." (I Timothy 4:1–2)

Unfortunately, this is common in today's Church. Jesus also teaches that as this is happening, there will be a great revival. He prophesied that in the last days a true Church would be birthed out of the church of man (religion) and that this Church would become a powerful movement through which thousands would come to know Jesus. As the difficulties prophesied take place, thousands will turn to God. Local churches will experience sudden and phenomenal growth as the Spirit of God is poured out on hungry people searching for truth.

It's a privilege to be part of this fulfilled prophecy. I currently serve on the pastoral staff at Destination Church in the Tri-Cities area of Virginia. Nine years ago, Destination was birthed in the hearts of my son Bryan and his wife, Kelly. In this short period, it has grown into a vibrant Pentecostal fellowship of more than three thousand. God daily confirms His Word and manifests His presence there with great miracles, signs, and wonders as prophesied both in the Old Testament and New.

Many involved in ministry and Church leadership today live in great expectation experiencing this phenomenal move of

God. Prophecy is being fulfilled before our very own eyes and we know His return is soon.

The third sign that Jesus gave was the overall condition of the world. He warned that we would experience a noted increase in world conflicts (wars) and rumors of wars. He further stated that we would see an increase in the number of and intensity of earthquakes and natural disasters. These would create a myriad of difficulties in daily life with widespread famine and worldwide pestilences (major social problems), which appear to have no easy solution.

Every culture in history has shared their own set of problems and difficulties. However, with all that is unfolding today, we live in a very different time. As I pen these meditations, the world is living under the horrific threat of a virus that is killing thousands. As a result we are required to quarantine in our homes and are not allowed to gather in public, not even in church. Life is changing and something definitive is going on.

Thankfully, as believers in Jesus Christ, we do not have to fear these days. We know Whom we believe in and our faith in Him and His Word will sustain and comfort us. Economically, environmentally, and socially, the world is on a collision course. All we can do is get out of the way and get into the Way, Jesus! He has warned us to prepare and said when all these things begin to happen, look up, for our redemption is coming.

The fourth and final sign Jesus taught to look for was the phenomenal changes that would take place in the earth with the weather during the last days. God is in charge of the weather and He has chosen to use it as a definitive sign of the end of times. "And there will be signs in the sun, and in the moon, and in the stars; and on the earth distress of nations, with perplexity, the sea and the waves roaring." (Luke 21:25)

The Secret Place

The most watched television personality in the world today is the local meteorologist. Every day we wake up and check what the forecast is and what changes we might be facing. There are uncharted climatic changes regularly taking place. We are experiencing devastating weather patterns that produce destructive storms all across our nation on almost a daily basis. They are increasing in both number and strength. National disasters that are staggering to our minds are creating havoc, with deaths and loss of property on a routine basis.

With all of our technological discoveries you would hope we could invent something to control or prevent these calamities. However, while man is good at predicting these events down to the specific location and hour, he is unable to control them. It reminds us how dependent we are on the mercy of God.

In one part of our nation there is record heat creating unbelievable drought sparking uncontrollable fires that ravage thousands of acres of precious forest and properties. It's killing crops, livestock, and human life. Just a few hours away, unprecedented storms create flood conditions that drive people from their homes. The end result is massive loss of property and loss of homes and human lives that can never be recovered.

Is all this just the result of climate change or could it be the Master of the climate and the world is attempting to get our full attention?

World leaders are exasperated. For decades, they've researched solutions to the mess we're in, but many are giving up, fearing there is no hope. War, conflict, mass murders, pandemics, political chaos, and economic collapse captivate headlines worldwide. Even secular scientists and world leaders predict Armageddon with a viewpoint that it is soon and unavoidable.

But for the Church and the family of God, this is our greatest hour and opportunity. We know the end of the story and our faith and future are secure in the hands of our God, who reigns over all. Each morning we wake in great expectation, knowing that this could be the day that Jesus comes. Our final exit is near and with joy unspeakable and full of glory.

"And when these things begin to come to pass, then look up, and lift up your heads; for your redemption draweth nigh." (Luke 21:28)

As we close this meditation, be encouraged not to give in to fear or anxiety. Our God is in control of it all. Prayerfully think on what we have shared here and allow the Holy Spirit to bring you comfort and peace. Keep your spiritual eyes open and your ears tuned, for the trumpet will sound!

"Therefore, beloved, looking forward to these things, be diligent to be found by Him in peace, without spot and blameless; and consider that the long-suffering of our Lord is salvation—as also our beloved brother Paul, according to the wisdom given to him, has written to you." (II Peter 3:14–15)

MEDITATION 6
THE LAST-DAY CHURCH (NEW WINE)

On the third day there was a wedding in Cana of Galilee, and the mother of Jesus was there. Now both Jesus and his disciples were invited to the wedding. And when they ran out of wine, the mother of Jesus said to Him, "They have no wine." Jesus said to her, "Woman, what does your concern have to do with me? My hour has not yet come." His mother said to the servants, "Whatever He says to you, do it." Now there were set there six waterpots of stone, according to the manner of purification of the Jews, containing twenty or thirty gallons apiece. Jesus said to them, "Fill the waterpots with water." And they filled them up to the brim. And He said to them, "Draw some out now, and take it to the master of the feast." And they took it. When the master of the feast had tasted the water that was made wine, and did not know where it came from (but the servants who had drawn the water knew), the master of the feast called the bridegroom. And he said to him, "Every man at the beginning sets out the good wine, and when the guests have well drunk, then the inferior. You have kept the good wine until now!" This beginning of signs Jesus did in Cana of Galilee, and manifested His glory; and His disciples believed in Him.

John 2:1–11

The Secret Place

In our previous meditation we learned what Jesus taught concerning God's defined timeline and the importance of discerning the times in which we now live. With this in mind, I want to explore what is prophesied about the Church of the last days in Scripture. It is absolutely crucial that you and I understand where we are and the all-important role we have in these special days.

In his last-day prophecy, the prophet Ezekiel saw a wheel within a wheel.

> *"Now as I looked at the living creatures, behold, a wheel was on the earth beside each living creature with its four faces. The appearance of the wheels and their workings was like the color of beryl, and all four had the same likeness. The appearance of their workings was, as it were, a wheel in the middle of a wheel." (Ezekiel 1:15–16)*

Today we are witnessing the birth of a Church out of the Church—a remnant who will faithfully serve the Lord, a remnant whose focus is on relationship with the living God rather than a religious system, the church of man. Hearing and understanding the Word of God demands a personal response from each of us. If we truly believe that the Bible is the uncompromised, inspired Word of God, then we will live in its truth and pattern our lives on the principles taught therein. If we choose to compromise and live by the world's standards, we will lose that divine revelation and the favor of our Heavenly Father.

Pay close attention to the exhortation from James, bishop of the early Church.

> *"Therefore lay aside all filthiness and overflow of wickedness, and receive with meekness the implanted Word, which is able to save*

your souls. But be doers of the Word, and not hearers only, deceiving yourselves." (James 1:21–22)

I encourage you to look inward and allow the Holy Spirit to conduct an inventory of your life, one that reveals where you are in your relationship with Jesus. It is not an easy task but incredibly necessary. As you sit prayerfully, quietly, with an open heart and mind in the secret place with our Heavenly Father, allow the Holy Spirit, who knows the hearts and minds of all, to search your heart and expose any attitude or activity that is not pleasing to our Father.

For His Church, these are intense days of disciplined preparation. Every revelation He gives us, every fulfilled prophecy, each sign and wonder is given for one purpose: to draw us closer to God and to lead us into a more intimate relationship with Him.

As stated earlier, after I was healed of Lewy body dementia and fully restored to life, God told Jane and me that the healing was for us, but the miracle was for others. Our Heavenly Father is reaching out to His family in these last days, drawing us unto Himself. In this sacred, secret place He delights in revealing Himself to us but more importantly He wants to reveal your heart to you. It is here that each of us must work out our own salvation as Paul spoke in Philippians 2:12.

Believing that we could be the Last-Day Church, there are two questions I wish to explore.

1. What is God doing with the Church?
2. What is the Church doing with God?

First, let's consider the prophetic picture given to us by John in his Gospel. Please re-read the text leading into this meditation (John 2:1–12). These verses show us the first public

The Secret Place

miracle Jesus performed. It was not by chance that Jesus began his public ministry by turning water into wine at a marriage feast. Neither was it simply His response to a need that caused Him to involve wine. God does everything in accordance with His divine plan and purpose. Therefore, everything Jesus said and did during His earthly ministry was in perfect harmony with His Father's will.

The incident at the wedding in Cana revealed the beginning of His ministry, while prophetically pointing to the end of His ministry. It speaks of the appointed time in which the Church, His bride, will be united with Him in eternal marriage at the end of time. Note that in the very beginning, Jesus refers to His Father's timeline.

When Jesus's mother approached Him on behalf of the wedded couple, Jesus responded, "My time has not yet come." Jesus was sensitive to His Father's plan and didn't do anything on His own accord. After His mother left, Jesus realized that it was His time. So He gladly helped this couple by providing wine for the celebration, taking advantage of the opportunity to do His Father's will.

Another interesting truth is found in Mary's response. "But His Mother told the servants, 'Do whatever He tells you.'" (verse 5) This response teaches the key to any miracle provision from God is to simply do what He tells you to do.

In the heart and mind of our Heavenly Father, obedience is of paramount importance. If we are to walk in His Spirit and receive His supernatural provision, we must live in total obedience to His will.

Another prophetic sign used here is revealed in the fact that Jesus used six stone waterpots instead of the traditional wineskins as was their custom. Wineskins could only serve a few guests, while waterpots were available to whoever wanted a drink. Why six and not one or five or seven? Why waterpots?

This points to God's plan for the End-Time Church. Remember, God created all things in six days. Therefore, it was prophetic that Jesus chose six water pots. He did so to signify the completion of His plan, to indicate that His rest would soon come. The new wine in the waterpots spoke of the new wine to be poured out upon all flesh (Joel 2) in the last days, when there is enough for whomever desires to drink.

Additionally, wine is often used to symbolize the Holy Spirit.

> *"See then that you walk circumspectly, not as fools but as wise, redeeming the time, because the days are evil. Therefore do not be unwise, but understand what the will of the Lord is. And do not be drunk with wine, in which is dissipation; but be filled with the Spirit." (Ephesians 5:15–17)*

In these last days our Heavenly Father is not only making available new wine, but He is also pouring it out in unmeasurable ways—not through the old wineskins of our traditions, but in an unprecedented manner. Anyone who thirsts can come into the secret place and drink as much as they desire.

> *"Nor do they put new wine into old wineskins, or else the wineskins break, the wine is spilled, and the wineskins are ruined. But they put new wine into new wineskins, and both are preserved." (Matthew 9:17)*

And just like at the wedding in Cana, the new wine is the best. As we say at Destination, the best is yet to come.

The Secret Place

Let me unwrap this powerful prophetic truth regarding the Last-Day Church. Jesus broke tradition by using stone waterpots instead of old wineskins. The new wine that God is pouring out on the world today cannot be contained in the old wineskins (traditions) of yesterday. God is doing a new work, preparing to take His people to a higher level.

For this stage of His divine plan we must be open minded and sensitive to the leading of the Holy Spirit. God is breaking us away from the old ways that we have become accustomed to in order to reach this present-day generation. In many areas it is uncomfortable, but if we allow the Holy Spirit to have His way, He will empower us to become life changers. We should be very careful in criticizing the new wine and its effects simply because it does not fit into our tradition or particular doctrinal beliefs.

Another insight is found in the response of the wedding's master of ceremony (verses 9–10). After tasting the new wine, he questioned the bridegroom for breaking tradition. Normally, the best wine would be served first then the weaker formula last. At this feast, the best was saved for last.

In essence the Master of Ceremony said, "No one has ever done it this way before." Sound familiar? Scripture teaches us that our Heavenly Father doesn't think as we do and His ways are often different than ours. Remember—Jesus taught that the first would be last and the last first. Should we be surprised that He saves the best wine for last? Of course not!

We also see this pattern in creation. God formed the earth with all the living plants and trees, then He populated it with animals and man. Lastly, He created woman. God often saves the best for last.

Elsewhere, God issued the covenant first to Abraham and the Jewish nation. He later established the new covenant through an incredible act of grace, the blood of Jesus.

> *"Is it not lawful for me to do what I wish with my own things? Or is your eye evil because I am good? So the last will be first and the first last. For many are called, but few are chosen." (Matthew 20:15–16)*

We shouldn't be surprised that the new wine Father provides today is better than the former. Unfortunately, so many in the Church today have the same problem as the guests at the wedding in Cana had. We have become so drunk on the wine from yesterday (traditions) that we have no appetite for the new. They have become so intoxicated on the traditions of their religion that they cannot and will not receive anything new, let alone acknowledge that it comes from our Heavenly Father.

Just as He did at the wedding in Cana, Jesus is doing things differently today and He has reserved the best for last. God is pouring new wine into new and different vessels but sadly, many good people reject it simply because it does not fit into their concept of Church or particular doctrine.

Many interpret this new move of God as a modern-day revival or a time of spiritual renewal. However, the Holy Spirit is showing me something more powerful. This new wine is more than a last-day revival, it is the last reformation!

If we Church leaders were totally honest, we would admit that the Church in America has largely become the church of man. We function under man-made rules of government, worship in shrines built by and to the glory of man (Luke 21), and plan our weekly services to please people. In essence, we have turned church into a spiritual supermarket catering to our every desire and need. And when God speaks, we're so focused on

The Secret Place

ourselves that we don't hear His voice.

That said, be careful you do not become spiritually gullible and accept everything you hear and see as being from God. At the same time, do not become so strong-willed and critical that you become close-minded. Remember that Jesus taught that His sheep will hear His voice (John 10:27). There are many false spirits, prophets, and teachers. As you cultivate intimacy with your Heavenly Father, He will keep you from falling into their traps.

How? By measuring everything by the Bible. If a teaching or experience cannot be found in Scripture, have nothing to do with it.

> *"Jesus said, 'If a son ask for bread from any father among you, will he give him a stone? Or if he asks for a fish, will he give him a serpent instead of a fish? Or if he ask for an egg, will he offer him a scorpion? If you then, being evil, know how to give good gifts to your children, how much more will your Heavenly Father give the Holy Spirit to those who ask Him!'" (Luke 11:11–13)*

Our Heavenly Father only gives His children the very best. He has reserved a new wine for the Last-Day Church (us) and this new wine is better than anything we have experienced. And instead of allowing drinking wine to excess and allowing it to damage our flesh, we ought to "be filled with the Spirit" (Ephesians 5:15–17). If we allow God to be God in us, He will make us more than conquerors, in every area of our lives.

To fully understand what God is doing with the Church today, consider the prophetic words given to Zechariah.

...

"Now the angel who talked with me came back and wakened me, as a man who is wakened out of his sleep. And he said to me, 'What do you see?' So I said, 'I am looking, and there is a lampstand of solid gold with a bowl on top of it, and on the stand seven lamps with seven pipes to the seven lamps. Two olive trees are by it, one at the right of the bowl and the other at its left.' So I answered and spoke to the angel who talked with me, saying, 'What are these, my lord?' Then the angel who talked with me answered and said to me, 'Do you not know what these are?' And I said, 'No my lord.' So he answered and said to me: 'This is the word of the Lord to Zerubbabel: "Not by might nor by power, but by my spirit" says the Lord of Host.'" (Zechariah 4:1–6)

Nothing can stand in the way of God's Church. We are the Lord's Army, empowered by His Spirit, and the gates of hell cannot stand against us!

MEDITATION 7
THE LAST-DAY CHURCH
(JESUS, WHERE ARE YOU?)

Now His parents went to Jerusalem every year at the Feast of the Passover. And when He was twelve years old, they went up to Jerusalem after the custom of the feast. And when they had fulfilled the days, as they returned, the child Jesus tarried behind in Jerusalem; and Joseph and His mother knew not of it. But they, supposing Him to have been in the company, went a day's journey; and they sought Him among their kinsfolk and acquaintances. And when they found Him not, they turned back again to Jerusalem, seeking Him. And it came to pass, that after three days they found Him in the temple, sitting in the midst of the doctors, both hearing them, and asking them questions. And all that heard were astonished at His understanding and answers. And when they saw Him, they were amazed; and His mother said unto Him, "Son, why hast thou thus dealt with us? Behold, thy father and I have sought thee sorrowing." And He said to them, "How is it that ye sought me? Wist ye not that I must be about my father's business?" And they understood not the saying which He spake unto them.

Luke 2:41–50

The Secret Place

In our final meditation, I want to seriously consider the question so many ask today: Jesus, where are you? Previously, I asked you to consider what God is doing with His Church today. Now, let's seek to discover what the Church is doing with Jesus.

Every truth that the Holy Spirit has taught us thus far brings us to this all-important question. Remember, we previously made a distinction between the church of man and the true Church that is being birthed out of man's religious systems. Once again, it is not my intention to be caustic or critical. What I am sharing, openly and honestly, comes from a grieved heart and great concern for all of God's people, living in this very critical time. It is not judgmental but a sincere, love-motivated warning to all God's family.

As difficult as it is to face the truth concerning the modern Church, it is past time to admit the spiritual realities that so clearly confront us. As His Church, we desperately need to pause and take a serious look inward and by so doing, ask the Holy Spirit to bring much needed conviction. Prayerfully consider what Jesus said in Matthew 13:14–17.

> *"And in them the prophecy of Isaiah is fulfilled, which says: 'Hearing you will hear and not understand, and seeing you will see and not perceive; for the hearts of this people have grown dull. Their ears are hard of hearing, and their eyes they have closed, lest they should see with their eyes and hear with their ears, lest they should understand with their hearts and turn, so that I should heal them.' But blessed are your eyes for they see, and your ears for they hear; for assuredly, I say to you that many prophets and righteous men desired to see what you see, and did not see it, and to hear what you hear, and did not hear it."*

Be warned! Many in these conflicting days will not hear what God is saying nor will they see what He is doing because they are blinded by the noise of this world and the tradition of man.

Jesus taught that the truth has the power to set us free. If we openly receive the conviction of the Holy Spirit in our lives and accept the loving correction of our Heavenly Father, He will heal our backsliding, deliver us from the bondage of this present world and rid us from the stench of religion. By so doing, we will acknowledge Christ's presence in His Church and most importantly, return Him to the throne of our hearts. Once again He will be our first love.

I encourage you to enter your prayer closet (the secret place) and meditate (think deeply) for a few moments, pondering the question, Jesus, where are you? To find our answer, let's unwrap the picture John saw at the beginning of the revelation God gave him while on the isle of Patmos.

John was "in the spirit" on the Lord's Day, and the Holy Spirit painted a very real picture that answered our question. As the same Holy Spirit illuminates this truth to our individual hearts, it is my prayer that each of us will respond with godly sorrow and a contrite spirit.

> *"To the angel of the Church of Ephesus write, 'These things says He who holds the seven stars in his right hand, who walks in the midst of the seven golden lampstands.'" (Revelation 2:1)*

> *"Behold, I stand at the door and knock. If anyone hears my voice and opens the door, I will come into him and dine with him, and he with Me." (Revelation 3:20)*

The Secret Place

A casual reading of these verses individually would cause us to miss the prophetic picture relating to the Last-Day Church (us). However, by prayerfully taking a closer look at these verses in context, when put alongside the previous story when Jesus's parents lost him, we see a clear answer to the question, Jesus, where are you?

Let's unwrap it together. The Apostle John, in prison on the isolated island of Patmos, received a revelation of Jesus Christ. He was instructed to write it down. He obeyed, and it is what we know as the book of Revelation. John saw things that had been, things that were happening in his day, and things that would happen to usher in the end of the world as we know it.

In the opening scenes of this prophetic vision, John is given a series of messages (Revelation 2 and 3) to the seven churches in Asia. Most Bible scholars agree that these messages were prophetic in content and directed to the End-Time Church as well. In Revelation, God begins this vision with a picture of where and what Jesus would be doing in the Church. The first thing we see is Jesus holding seven stars in His right hand. Remember that seven is God's number for completion. These stars are symbolic of the messengers to the churches.

Noting what John wrote in Revelation 1:6, that each of us have been made kings and priests (messengers) unto God, we gain great comfort. Jesus is holding us in His right hand! This is exactly where He is in these horrific days—holding us in His right hand of strength and power.

> *"And I give them eternal life, and they shall never perish; neither shall anyone snatch them out of my hand. My Father, who has given them to Me, is greater than all; and no one is able to snatch them out of my Father's hand. I and my Father are one." (John 10:28–30)*

God has everything under control and our future is as bright as the Son Himself. "He is our refuge and strength, a very present help in trouble." (Psalm 46:1)

Now, let's continue by noting the second picture that John saw in Revelation 2:1: Jesus walking in the midst of the seven golden lampstands. We are told that these lampstands are symbolic of the seven Churches. Where is Jesus? In the midst of His Church.

When we study the messages given to each of these churches, we see a common pattern and purpose that speaks prophetically to the Last-Day Church. Five of the seven letters begin with a commendation for the good that the Church is doing. Next, there is a clear and frank exposure of what is wrong in the Church. Then He offers a solution, a loving correction that shows how to resolve that wrong. Interestingly, He closes each message with the same exhortation: "Let them who have ears, hear what the Spirit is saying to the Church."

This clearly presents His purpose in the Church. We are His bride and He is present to bring comfort, conviction, and correction. It is interesting that He gave this picture at the beginning of the Revelation.

The third and final picture is seen at the end of these seven messages. Understanding their prophetic emphasis, we must take to heart that this is the last word from God to His Church, just prior to the rapture.

In the beginning, Jesus holds us in His right hand, as He walks in the midst of the Church. Here, in Revelation 3:20, we see an entirely different picture, but part of the same message. If you listen carefully and allow the Holy Spirit to anoint your eyes to see clearly, the picture is quite disturbing. In my opinion, this is one of the most misapplied verses in the Bible. Commonly

The Secret Place

used during altar calls, the verse is framed as a plea for people to open their hearts and let Jesus come "in." Certainly, Jesus desires that, but when we use this verse in that context, we miss the real picture that the Holy Spirit gave John.

John did not see Jesus knocking on the door of a man's heart. He saw Jesus standing at the door of the Church, trying to enter! Like Jesus's parents at Passover, we have become so busy doing religious things that we shut Him out, and tragically, we don't even know it. And as it was in the day of Noah, the only door handle to open the door is on the inside. Jesus is on the outside, trying to get our attention. He cries, "If just one of you will open the door, I will come in and fellowship with you."

Is it really possible? Is it conceivable that in all of our religiosity, even with the best of intentions, we have left Him outside without even realizing it? We keep preaching, prophesying, praying, singing, dancing, and worshiping, not realizing that He is missing. We must stop doing this and start being the Church by giving Him His rightful place, as the focus of every song, sermon, and program.

Mary and Joseph lost Jesus, and they lost Him in the Church. Have we fallen into the same trap? We build our million-dollar buildings and furnish them with the best and most current technologies. Our worship teams spend hours practicing to perform a flawless service, and we plan every moment from beginning to benediction.

I cry out to you not in criticism nor fiery judgment, but with a broken heart. Let's get serious with God and allow Him to turn on the searchlight of the Holy Spirit to reveal what we need to reach this generation for Jesus. Prayer can no longer be replaced with programs and endless practices. We need to humble ourselves and cry out to God and open the doors to our hearts and His Church. Will you open the door and invite Him in? Can you hear His knock? His cry? Scripture teaches that He will appear unto them who look for Him a second time. Are you looking?

Serving His servants,

Pastor Larry